Published by Shadow River Books
King George, Virginia
Text and pictures copyright 2024 by Debra Hewitt.
All rights reserved. This book in whole or in part may not be reproduced in any form without permission in writing from the publisher.

Books ordered online are shipped directly from the printer. Please request a replacement for a book which seems defective.

The author gratefully acknowledges the use of personal photographs in preparing these illustrations. Many, many thanks to the family pictured here for their trust and participation!

And many thanks to my husband and daughters for their support and suggestions as I created this book.
I could not have done this without you!

ISBN: 978-1-945472-24-4 (hardcover)
ISBN: 978-1-945472-22-0 (paperback)
ISBN: 978-1-945472-23-7 (epub)

If you enjoy this book, please consider leaving a review online or sharing about it on social media.

Visit www.shadowriverbooks.com to request a recording of this book and check availability in other languages.

For Atticus and Isaac,
who inspired this book.

I hope you will always cherish
the special bond of being brothers!

When you have a brother...

or even just hanging around the house.

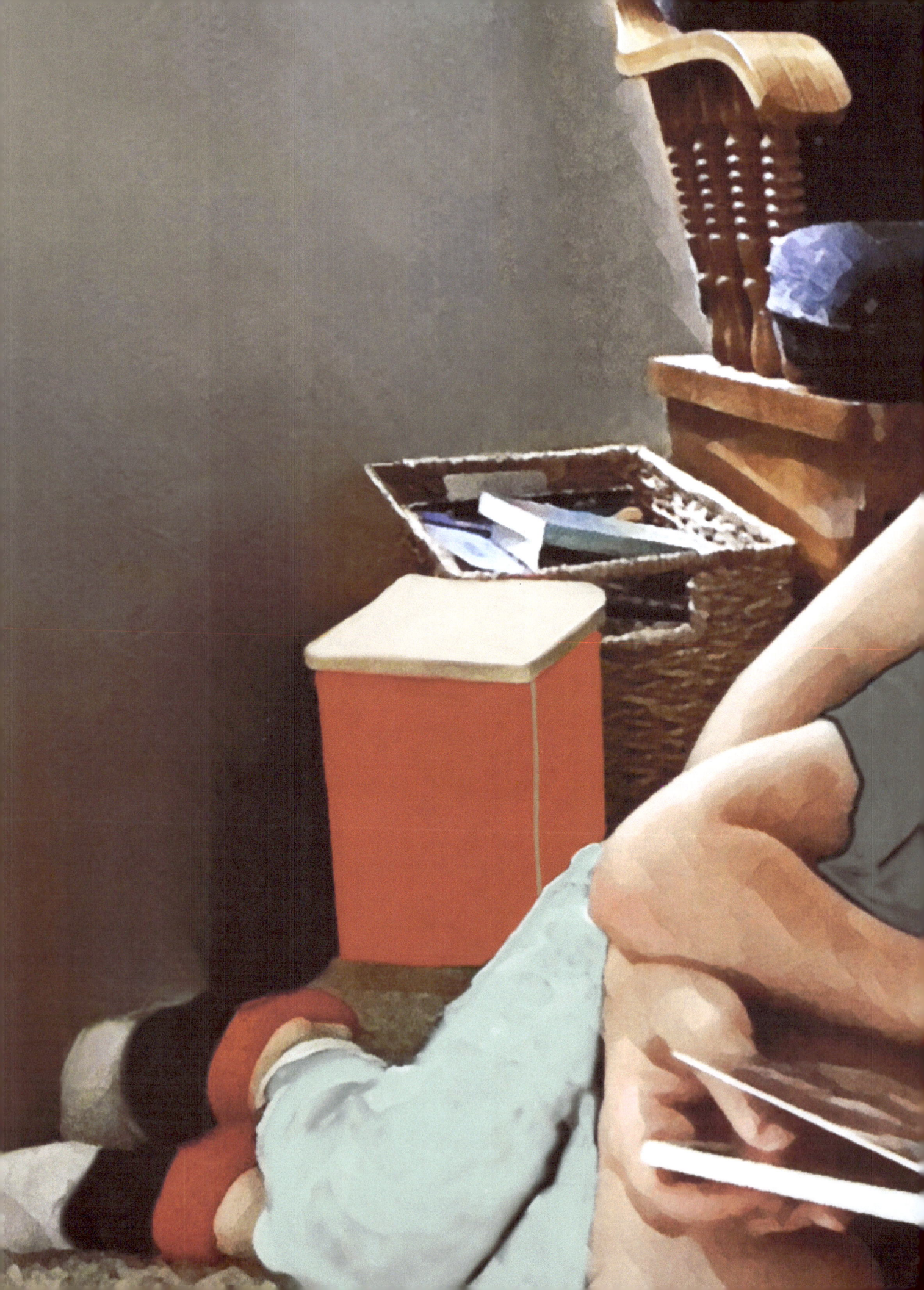

a story,
or a lap.

If you have a big brother, you have someone to watch out for you and keep you safe.

If you have a little brother, you have someone who looks up to you and cheers you on.

In good times or bad—

when you're happy—

or sad—

a brother teaches you how to love.

www.ingramcontent.com/pod-product-compliance
Lightning Source LLC
Chambersburg PA
CBHW050752110526
44592CB00002B/40